# CURRANTS, OLIVES & COTTON
## HISTORY OF THE IONIAN BANK

### Ian Moncrief-Scott

Information Management Solutions Limited

ISLE OF MAN

The author Ian Moncrief-Scott has asserted his right under the Copyright, Designs and Patents Act 1988 to be identified as the author of this work.

Copyright. © I. Moncrief-Scott 2021

All rights reserved. No part of this publication may be produced in any form or by any means - graphic, electronic, or mechanical, including photocopying, recording, taping, or information storage and retrieval systems - without the prior permission in writing of the publishers.

The publishers make no representation, express or implied, regarding the accuracy of the information contained in this book and cannot accept any legal responsibility for any errors or omissions that may take place.

A CIP catalogue record for this book is available from the British Library.

Published by Information Management Solutions Limited, 17 Howe Road, Onchan, Isle of Man, IM3 2BB.

Printed, bound and distributed by IngramSpark.

Book Layout © 2017 BookDesignTemplates.com

Superhero Peg Image: Besjunior/Shutterstock.com

Cover Source by Tanja Prokop of BookDesignTemplates.com

**CURRANTS, OLIVES & COTTON: HISTORY OF THE IONIAN BANK - 1st ed.**
ISBN 9781903467077

The Publishers have been requested by the author to acknowledge the direct and indirect contributions to this book by The Ionian Bank.

This book is dedicated to
start-up entrepreneurs.


The front cover depicts
ordinary wooden clothes pegs dressed as
Super Heroes.


**All start-up entrepreneurs are
ordinary people
turning into Super Heroes!**

# CONTENTS

CURRANTS, OLIVES & COTTON ...... 8
BIBLIOGRAPHY ...... 19
OTHER BOOKS BY THE AUTHOR ...... 21
FORTHCOMING BOOKS BY THE AUTHOR ...... 22

# CURRANTS, OLIVES & COTTON

Languishing in the azure Mediterranean Sea, the picturesque Ionian Isles seem an unlikely venue for vast international trade and the spread of Mexican dollars.

Undoubtedly, early links with Venice helped, but the influences of France, Turkey, Britain and, ultimately, Greece have left indelible marks.

In 1814, occupying French forces abandoned Corfu. Soon after the Napoleonic collapse, Ionia found itself hosting a 'protector', a Lord High Commissioner, courtesy of Great Britain.

Currants and olive oil provided an economic backbone. Currency was mainly coin, comprising silver dollars and Mexican and Maria Theresa thalers.

By 1825 Britain sought to determine Sterling as the unifying standard.

Credit hardly existed in this agricultural community. Poor, unorganised peasants suffered harshly under the dominance of monopolistic merchants. Meagre loans demanded usurious interest.

A cash society created other problems. Lord Nugent, The High Commissioner, remarked, "the keeping and secreting in private houses numerous and sometimes vast amounts of specie, which occasioned frequent predatory and frightful incursions from the Barbarians of Albania.

Commodity prices plummeted in the early 1830s through the Gold Standard's return, creating massive deflation. Former French occupiers had wreaked a legacy of havoc on indigenous output by squandering huge swathes of life-preserving olive groves and currant bushes for firewood. 25-30% interest rates were commonplace.

Farmers neared ruin.

Lord Nugent had a plan. Gold and silver hoards must be enticed into the open. He established a £35,000 fund with an interest rate of 6% for farming loans ahead of harvest. It was a huge success, much to the chagrin of merchants and moneylenders.

Inspired, he pursued the notion of a national fund and even local paper currency. It would stimulate the movement of capital and safely reward the Treasury.

Sadly, London scorned the concept.

The Lords Commissioners declared it "would most particularly and decidedly object to a British Government being considered in many ways responsible for any description of paper currency issued by the Government of the Ionian Islands" Lord Nugent resigned.

Mindful of his predecessor's mistakes, Sir Howard Douglas assumed the reins of power. He abandoned the national loan scheme and was careful not to be drawn into the rows.

Eventually, life on the Island mellowed his demeanour. Sir Douglas issued the vital recommendation for a United Ionian States Bank with powers for agricultural loans, pawnbroking and deposit-taking.

This time, London was more responsive. Perhaps, competitive threats of proposed Gibraltar and Malta Banks helped?

Subscription of four thousand £25 shares was planned for Island launch in 1837. Local Government would hold one-sixth, in return for a proportionate right to appoint directors. The response was poor.

Immediately, the project died.

The revival was equally swift. London became the focus of capital search. Ionian States London Agent, Sir Alexander Wood, formulated proposals for the Ionian State Bank.

Start-up capital was again £100,000 in £25 shares and the Bank was to be prescribed under Ionian State law with limited Ionian liability.

Key was the growing trade with Britain. "The Ionian Islands are so advantageously situated with respect to the Mediterranean, the Adriatic and the Levant, that the operations of the Bank are capable of easy and advantageous extension over a wide range, and thus the project established may be the nucleus of a great and important undertaking," heralded the glowing prospectus.

New offices at Aldermanbury, London, quickly bore the Minute Book's first entry. 1 March 1839, "the sum of £14,000 was lent to Messrs. John Wright & Co., Bankers, at 5% on the security of Florida Bonds, the loan subject to the call for payment at a fortnight's notice."

Later that month, two envoys, Mr. J Hunter and Mr. S Ward were despatched to Corfu. Their mission – smooth operations and report progress. Early news was not good. Opposition was formidable. Though this was not the fault of the Bank, anti-British sentiment was growing.

The Ionian Parliament was dissolved.

Formative months at the Bank had been rough. But, an ingenious solution was to hand. Since the former Legislative Authority enacted an 1837 law for a local bank, which had failed, the two men successfully lobbied that a new local institution should be automatically approved.

On 23 October 1939, The Ionian Bank, having lost the word 'State' during Senate debate, finally emerged as a Joint Stock Company. Interestingly, the name-change did not appear in the Minute Book.

Exclusive rights for note issue were granted for twenty years.

Operations commenced.

All was now in place.

Minutes of 30 December 1839, recorded "resolved that £5000 in British specie be sent out to Corfu by the Packet of the 18 January and that Mr. Ward be authorized to issue drafts on the Bank to the extent of £10,000."

On 2 March 1840, the Bank opened in Corfu. Zante followed on 18 May, Kephalonia by 10 August 1840. 'This Infant Ionian Institution', as it was known in Memoranda of the day between London and the Islands, suffered much petty and vindictive opposition.

Local prejudice, coupled with political unrest, continued. It was hardly surprising that the local Treasurer General was particularly difficult. Until the Bank's launch and despite being a public servant, he had provided private loans and deposits, using the local military safe.

In time, the Bank was able to demonstrate the economic improvements it had brought to the Islands. Opposition evaporated.

However, the Bank still did not have the necessary status in England. Despite the Deed of Settlement, which had permitted operations in the Islands, no such rights existed in Great Britain.

When the Ionian Bank requested an account with Bankers, Messrs. Smith, Payne and Smith, they were formally rebuffed for lack of a proper Charter. An account titled, W. Brown and others, saved their public embarrassment. (Mr. William Brown was a director). Fortunately, a Royal Charter arrived in January 1844.

After the Bank of England, The Ionian Bank's Royal Charter is listed third.

The early years continued to be eventful as the Bank financed growing trade between the Islands and Britain.

Currency fluctuation provided an immediate danger.

With Mexican dollars flowing freely through the Islands, a devaluation in 1844 was met by a Branch Bank Inspector's instruction that "all his payments must be in the sterling value and that discounting any bills care must be taken to make them payable in sterling and to keep as small a stock of Mexican dollars as possible."

Business development continued, with agencies in Patras and Athens to handle the growing ties with Greece. Agents were appointed in Trieste and Venice. Correspondent relationships grew across Europe. Storms beckoned.

Political upheaval reigned in Europe in 1848. Loyal merchants narrowly avoided a run on the Kephalonia branch. A mob attacked Patras, only to be repulsed thanks to HMS Spitfire, Royal Navy. The crop failure in 1851 caused widespread panic in Corfu, wiping out several merchants.

A similar 1857 run and the loss of the currant harvest Zante & Kephalonia were successfully weathered. The Bank's esteem grew. A 20-year licence extension rewarded its care. Under the permit, the Bank Inspector and the Chief Manager had to reside permanently in Corfu. Now the Bank was their own.

Great Britain gave up her sovereignty of the Islands to the Kingdom of Greece in 1864. A new charter changed the Bank to Societe Anonyme and the Government assumed debt responsibilities. Agencies in Athens and Patras developed into formal branches, and in 1873, Athens became HQ.

With the Drachma, as Greece's currency and the Bank still able to issue its own notes, friction was inevitable.

Mr. J Horatio Lloyd resolved the conflict following lengthy and delicate discussions. The Bank would retain its monopoly in the Islands and could expand into Greece, provided the National Bank consented to any new branch where it already had a presence.

Relations flourished and were strengthened to repel the Greek Government's declaration that it would issue notes itself. Within a week, it withdrew.

By granting the Banks increased note-issuing powers and removing obligations to redeem notes in specie, the Government gained a loan of 21 million Drachmas.

Now the Bank's notes were legal tender.

Cautiously the Bank increased its business.

This prudence was to pay dividends when the Greek Government suspended cash payments twice in seven years.

Meanwhile, in Britain, the Bank decided to change to a Joint Stock Company and, in 1883, surrendered its Royal Charter.

The Bank retained its Greek Charter until 1905, though a Special 1880 Law did remove its note-issue monopoly in the Islands. But, for the first time, as a Bank of Issue, the Ionian Bank now equalled the National Bank of Greece.

However, the euphoria looked short-lived. Over the coming years, the National Bank of Greece pressed hard to drive political will to cancel dual-issuing authority.

In 1902, a strong Bank team went to lobby for a renewal of its powers. Opposition was formidable and the venture seemed lost before it commenced.

With the support of Sir Edwin Egerton, British Minister in Greece, and the Bank's overwhelming esteem in the Islands, they won the day against all the odds.

A Royal Decree sealed rights for another 15- year maximum.

Though the Bank did try to sell the issue rights to the National Bank before maturity, a forceful Greek shareholder revolt ensured they remained for the term.

With the impending loss of profitable note-issue, new markets needed to be found. Egypt was chosen. Many Greeks lived there and it was a short southward journey. More importantly, the cotton trade boomed.

A branch opened in Alexandria in 1907. Despite some difficult years, because of the unpredictable reliance on the single crop of cotton, the Bank prospered.

Crop movement and cultivation became specialist areas of investment. Buying and selling formed important income, especially as the Bank pretended to be only an agent. By the 1920s, the Bank was the leading institution handling cotton arrival in Alexandria.

Two world wars tested the Bank.

Although London had frozen all liquid assets, the Bank of England did help offset the withdrawal panic sweeping Greece by honouring due bills.

Throughout the conflict, the Bank helped the Allies in the Balkans and even Turkey's war with Greece had little impact.

In 1922, The Ionian Bank acquired the Guaranty Trust Company of New York's branch in Constantinople.

Even with hopes that when peace returned, it would support business between Turkey and Egypt, seven years later, it closed.

A venture into Cyprus proved much more successful. The Ionian Bank was the first British bank in the country. Five branches quickly spanned the Island.

During 1938, the Bank formed the Ionian Insurance Company and began to acquire Banque Populaire of Greece's 'Big Five'. Germans and Italians had other ideas.

Bank assets were sequestrated.

Banque Populaire became Italian and German insurance companies swallowed the Ionian arm. Many branches were physically damaged.

Although Greek business stood still, the remarkable forethought of the Egyptian venture proved lifesaving. British guarantees for the cotton crop, and huge Allied military spending, surged the market.

Hostilities ceased.

The Ionian ventures were successfully disentangled but the old Drachma was destroyed. Each new Drachma replaced 50 million old ones.

The economy struggled.

By 1952 normality had begun to return, bolstered by the Central Bank of Greece's bold fiscal initiatives.

Today, despite becoming the Ionian and Popular Bank of Greece SA in February 1958, the recent acquisition by Alpha Bank AE, Athens has condemned the name to the mists of time.

The London Branch of the Ionian Bank was bought by Commercial Bank of Greece and opened as a full branch in April 2000.

# BIBLIOGRAPHY

Ionian Bank. (1953). *The Ionian Bank - A History*. London: The Ionian Bank.

# OTHER BOOKS BY THE AUTHOR

As Good As Gold - History of Pound Sterling. ISBN 0-9534818-4-0

Currants, Olives & Cotton (eBook). ISBN 9781903467169

De La Rue Straw Hats to Global Securities. ISBN 0- 9534818-2-4

Euro History & Development. ISBN 0-9534818-1-6

Holidays 2000 – A Time Capsule. ISBN 0-9534818-7-5

Negotiate to Win! - The Introductory Edition. ISBN 0-9534818-6-7

Start Any Business (Print). ISBN 9781903467008
Start Any Business (eBook). ISBN 9781903467015

Scripophily - Historic Bond & Share Collecting. ISBN 0-9534818-5-9

The Eternal Old Lady - Bank of England. ISBN 0-9534818-3-2

The Green Shoots of Money (Print). ISBN 9781903467107
The Green Shoots of Money (eBook). ISBN 9781903467114

The Hitmen - Part One. ISBN 0-9534818-8-3

# FORTHCOMING BOOKS BY THE AUTHOR

As Good As Gold (Print). ISBN 9781903467039
As Good As Gold (eBook). ISBN 9781903467121

De La Rue (Print). ISBN 9781903467046
De La Rue (eBook). ISBN 9781903467138

Euro (Print). ISBN 9781903467053
Euro (eBook). ISBN 9781903467145

Scripophily (Print). ISBN 9781903467084
Scripophily (eBook). ISBN 9781903467176

Tail-less Cats & Three-legged Men (Print). ISBN 9781903467091
Tail-less Cats & Three-legged Men (eBook). ISBN 9781903467183

The Eternal Old Lady (Print). ISBN 9781903467060
The Eternal Old Lady (eBook). ISBN 9781903467152

## ABOUT THE AUTHOR

Ian Moncrief-Scott has over fifty years of broad business experience, mostly gained at international level, based in the UK.

As a former senior executive for a global publishing and information technology company headquartered in the USA, he has contributed to numerous client-facing procurement and outsourcing initiatives worldwide.

Ian has created and participated in numerous small businesses in the UK, Isle of Man and elsewhere.

He has also represented the Isle of Man Government Department for Enterprise in several of its business support schemes. Ian designed and delivered extensive training for its Micro Business Grant Scheme.

In recognition of his long-term service to the Department, Ian was nominated for The Queen's Award for Enterprise Promotion and awarded an official Certificate of Recognition in 2018.

Throughout his career, he has maintained an active interest in start-ups, especially those involving the financial sector.

At the turn of the millennium, several of the articles written by Ian that form this short work were originally published by the Museum of American Financial History (now the Museum of American Finance).

www.ingramcontent.com/pod-product-compliance
Lightning Source LLC
Chambersburg PA
CBHW071722080526
44588CB00012B/1869